THE LIGH

*for Jess.
with
love
xx.*

BY THE SAME AUTHOR

POETRY

The hoop
Common Knowledge
Feast Days
The Myth of the Twin
Swimming in the Flood
A Normal Skin
The Asylum Dance

FICTION

The Dumb House
The Mercy Boys
Burning Elvis
The Locust Room

THE LIGHT TRAP

John Burnside

CAPE POETRY

Published by Jonathan Cape 2002

2 4 6 8 10 9 7 5 3

Copyright © John Burnside 2002

John Burnside has asserted his right under the Copyright, Designs
and Patents Act 1988 to be identified as the author of this work

This book is sold subject to the condition that it shall not,
by way of trade or otherwise, be lent, resold, hired out,
or otherwise circulated without the publisher's prior
consent in any form of binding or cover other than that
in which it is published and without a similar condition
including this condition being imposed on the
subsequent purchaser

First published in Great Britain in 2002 by
Jonathan Cape
Random House, 20 Vauxhall Bridge Road,
London SW1V 2SA

Random House Australia (Pty) Limited
20 Alfred Street, Milsons Point, Sydney,
New South Wales 2061, Australia

Random House New Zealand Limited
18 Poland Road, Glenfield,
Auckland 10, New Zealand

Random House South Africa (Pty) Limited
Endulini, 5A Jubilee Road, Parktown 2193, South Africa

The Random House Group Limited Reg. No. 954009
www.randomhouse.co.uk

A CIP catalogue record for this book
is available from the British Library

ISBN 0 224 06177 1

Papers used by Random House are natural,
recyclable products made from wood grown in sustainable forests;
the manufacturing processes conform to the environmental
regulations of the country of origin

Typeset by Palimpsest Book Production Limited,
Polmont, Stirlingshire
Printed and bound in Great Britain by
Biddles Ltd, Guildford and King's Lynn

for Sarah and Lucas

A man and a woman
Are one.
A man and a woman and a blackbird
Are one.
                    Wallace Stevens

CONTENTS

I HABITAT

Koi	3
Taxonomy	6
Deer	10
Harunobu: 'Catching Fireflies'	12
Field Mice	15
Animism	16
Being and Time	17
Animals	18
History	20

II Φυσις

The Light Trap	23
Heat Wave	26
Another poem about fish	28
The Gravity Chair	30
Dürer's 'Rhinoceron'	31
The Emporium of Light	32
Milgram's 'Shock Generator'	33
Of gravity and light	34
History	40

III WORLD

Birth Songs	45
Kith	52
On Kvaloya	53

A Duck Island flora	59
Bleik	60
Blackbird	63
After Lucretius	70
Viriditas	78
A theory of everything	83

ACKNOWLEDGEMENTS

Acknowledgements are due to the editors of the following: *Birdsuit, Guardian, London Review of Books, New Yorker, Pretext* and *The Times Literary Supplement*.

HABITAT

What is meant here is something more mutually and functionally interdependent between mind and terrain, an organic relationship between the environment and the unconscious, the visible space and the conscious, the ideas and the creatures.

Paul Shepard

KOI

The trick is to create a world
from nothing

        – not the sound a blackbird makes
in drifted leaves

not dogwood
        or the unexpected scent
of jasmine by the west gate

            not the clouds
reflected in these puddles all around
the bowling green
        deserted after rain
and darker than an early polaroid –

but nothing
        which is present in the flesh
as ripeness is: a lifelong urgency.

The trick is in the making
        not the made

beginning where an idle mind spools out
to borderline and limit
        half a mile
of shadow in the pine woods
        or a rim

of wetland – rush and willow
gathered close
        like mourners in the dark –

            a sudden
ambiguity of liverwort or birch

suggesting no man's land
                      or journey's end.

As everything is given
                and conceived
imagined real
        a stone's throw in the mind

it's not the thing itself
                but where it stands

– the shadows fanned
                or dripping from a leaf
the gap between each named form and the next

where frogs and dragonflies arrive
from nowhere
            and the kingdom is at hand
in every shift of colour and degree

bullfinch and squirrel
              hawk-moth
and antirrhinum.

All afternoon we've wandered from the pool
to alpine beds and roses
                and the freshly-painted
palm house

        all afternoon
we've come back to this shoal
of living fish.

Crimson and black
            pearl-white
                      or touched with gold
the koi hang in a realm of their invention

with nothing that feels like home
                              – a concrete pool
and unfamiliar plants spotted with light
birdsong and traffic
                  pollen and motes of dust

and every time the veil above their heads
shivers into noise
                  they dart
and scatter

            though it seems more ritual now
than lifelike fear
                  as if they understood
in principle
            but couldn't wholly grasp

the vividness of loss

and every time we gaze into this pool
of bodies
      we will ask

how much they know of us
                              and whether this
is all illusion

            like the play of light
across a surface gilded with a drift
of pollen

            or the sound a blackbird makes
as it withdraws
                  one moment at a time

remembering its myth of origin.

TAXONOMY

for Linda Gregerson

I FLORA

Because it can only be shared,
like a waltz,
or trust,

this commonplace affection singles out
a hairstreak,
or the pattern on a leaf,

leaving the rest untold;
the world
unspoken;

and though we mostly look
for what we know,
there is something we love in ourselves

that a meadow answers:
the blue of an upland flower
or a tideline of grass;

the heart-shaped
or spatulate leaf
of toadflax, or fern.

The colour
is nothing like baize
or polished jade;

the gap between coltsfoot and mint
no more or less
specific than a kale field after rain,

but looking always worked towards a word:
trading the limits of speech
for the unsaid presence,

the way the bird
that vanished through the leaves
is true forever now, being unseen,

and the magic
that speech performs
is all

continuum: the given and the named
discovered and invented
one more time,

with each new bud or tendril that unfolds
upon the revelation
of the known.

II FAUNA

Once we are close enough to give them names
we cannot help but treat them as our own,
these animals;

though they are far from us, and rapt
in other frequencies,
like waves, or stars,

we speak as if they understood the words,
as if this fondness
were the only language.

They say, in the earliest myth,
before the descent,
our father Orpheus would sometimes charm

new creatures from the air: musk-ox and deer
pressed into life
and ringed about with song.

I always think of them as privileged,
enchanted by the intimate surprise
of other bodies; yet they might have been

uncertain of the presence they possessed,
the fresh light singling them out, like revenants,
as they took form

and shaped a chiming world.
It's difficult not to think in *déja-vu*
when everything seems so familiar

– wisteria; lilac; the century plant in bloom
like a pillar of salt –
difficult not to believe we might go down

amongst the shadows, stealing love from time
and coming home
to where the song begins

as if this world were nothing but a gap,
the afterlife of dust and locust trees
we used to imagine in school, or that cursive space

where one form is abandoned for the next:
the old flesh invested with snow
and the taste of currants;

the old regrets and loves becoming
tendons; milk-teeth;
misted fingerprints.

DEER

*of your charity disturb them not
in their Arcadia*
                    F. Fraser Darling

Coming inside from a meal
in the garden, the lights burning out
on the table, a threadlike spill
of maple syrup warming in the dark
to draw some passing creature to this quiet
theatre of crockery and fruit-bowls and the last
glimmer of chablis amongst the pears,

we wonder about those legends
of women transformed into deer,
or a cold daughter, lost in the hills
and hidden in the caught breath of a fawn.

Imagine how they slip between two lives
in skipping rhymes; how they recall
the water in the fern, or wintersweet
unfurling on the tongue's unfinished skin;
how, when they steal in through the cypress hedge
to such a feast, they catch a thread of musk
and see themselves again, in human form.

Sometimes I have waited at the edge
of darkness for a glimpse of something wild
and mutable, a sweet glitch in the tale
to show the borderland through which they pass,

and if I could have chosen anything
but this inevitable self, I'd be the one
who walks alone and barefoot in the woods

to stand, amidst a family of deer,
knowing her kind, and knowing the chasm between
one presence and the next as nothing more
than something learned, like memory, or song.

HARUNOBU: 'CATCHING FIREFLIES'

Because what they love
is gravity itself

– the echo of a struck bell,
or the splash

a bowl makes, as it falls
and shatters;

because they love
the turning of the tide

and how the current
shapes itself to fit

the swimmer as he drifts
towards the shore,

reluctant to let him go,
sounding him out,

then running on
with something

clean
and weighted

printed
in the flow;

because they love
the fixity of things,

the soft pull of the earth,
the roots of song,

they go out to the lake,
with nets and traps,

to capture light
and hold it in a box.

I remember shining a torch
at a moonless sky,

knowing that feeble ray
would travel on

for all eternity, through
space and time,

more permanent
than anything

I thought about
as matter.

And even though
we picture them

as half-lives
– fireflies, creatures of a day –

I guess these sparks
of flesh

and brilliance,
having shone,

will never cease from being,
never dim,

although their handmade cages
keep them

wedded to the earth,
as gravity

makes light
material: a local tide

we salvage
from the instantaneous

in marsh-grass, lilies,
glimmers of bamboo.

FIELD MICE

I think of them as guests.
The closest we come to wild, on this tidy street,
that odour in the shed
like hemlock, or these shreds
of paper, where we once had bulbs, or seeds;

the glide of skin and bone across a floor
recurring, in a half-forgotten dream
for weeks, no more
substantial than the wind we listen for
through talk-shows and the news; a hidden stream

of warmth and dread, alive beneath the home
we only half possess, sharing their fear,
as if our lives were scribbled on the air
or ciphered in the dust
like musk, or spoor.

ANIMISM

As if this house contained
a secret animal,
I keep watch, while I lie awake at night,
remembering your father's
bible, like a newly-gutted fish,
open forever
at Leviticus,

and how you always verged upon
the older forms of prayer,
unveiling bees and starlings in the roof,
lacewings and frogs, that aftermath of grin
and civet you discovered in a trap,
quiet as dust
beneath the outhouse floor,

how every small erasure
in the snow
was dreamed to life
as something you could hear:
a thin song in the walls; a narrow purl
of infant longing
built into the stair.

BEING AND TIME

There are times when I think
of the knowledge we had as children:

the patterns we saw in number, or the spells
and recipes we had
for love and fear;

the knowledge we kept in the bones
for wet afternoons,
the slink of tides, the absolutes of fog,

or how a lapwing's egg can tip
the scale of the tongue;

how something was always present in the snow
that fell between our parish and the next,

a perfect thing, not what was always there,
but something we knew without knowing, as we knew

that everything was finite and alive,
cradled in warmth against the ache of space,

marsh-grass and shale, and the bloodroot we dug in the woods
that turned our fingers red, and left a stain

we kept for weeks, through snow and miles of sleep,
as if it was meant to happen, a sliver of fate
unstitching its place in the marrow, and digging in.

ANIMALS

for Allison Funk

There are nights when we cannot name
the animals that flit across our headlights,

even on moonlit journeys, when the road
is eerie and still

and we smell the water long before
the coast road, or those lamps across the bay,

they cross our path, unnameable and bright
as any in the sudden heat of Eden.

Mostly, it's rabbit, or fox, though we've sometimes caught
a glimpse of powder blue, or Chinese white,

or chanced upon a mystery of eyes
and passed the last few miles in wonderment.

It's like the time our only neighbour died
on Echo Road,

leaving her house unoccupied for months,
a darkness at the far end of the track

that set itself apart,
the empty stairwell brooding in the heat,

the blank rooms filling with scats
and the dreams of mice.

In time, we came to think that house contained
a presence: we could see it from the yard

shifting from room to room in the autumn rain
and we thought it was watching us: a kindred shape

more animal than ghost.
They say, if you dream an animal, it means

'the self' – that mess of memory and fear
that wants, remembers, understands, denies,

and even now, we sometimes wake from dreams
of moving from room to room, with its scent on our hands

and a slickness of musk and fur
on our sleep-washed skins,

though what I sense in this, and cannot tell
is not the continuity we understand

as self, but life, beyond the life we live
on purpose: one broad presence that proceeds

by craft and guesswork,
shadowing our love.

HISTORY

*As a simplistic, linear, literal account of events and powers
as unpredictable as parental anger, history is a juvenile idea.*
                                            Paul Shepard

Then Adam forgot the names and one by one
the creatures died.

He seemed heroic then, a breed apart,
and how he loved them more for being lost

became his only myth, a tale he told
of golden frogs and blood-red simians.

Sometimes he wondered if they died en masse
or if a single female had remained

for months in the forest,
lamenting the loss of her kind.

And this was how he knew himself at last,
the unvoiced presence shining in his eyes

made flesh again, made whole, untouched by god,
and homesick for the other animals.

Miss Waldron's Red Colobus, 12th September 2000

II

Φυσις

The only laws of matter are those which our minds must fabricate, and the only laws of mind are fabricated for it by matter.

James Clerk Maxwell

φυσις κρυπτεσθαι φιλει

Heraclitus

THE LIGHT TRAP

I

Homesick for the other animals,
at midnight, in the soft midsummer dark,
we rigged a sail of light amidst
the apple trees beyond your mother's lawn
and counted moths.

This was our first experiment
in guesswork, with a car-torch and a stolen
bedsheet from the upstairs linen press:
our faces smudged with shadow in the lucent
undergrowth, the powder on our wrists

subtle and sweet as graphite, as we named
the shapes we recognised: Merveille-du-jour;
Sycamore; Mother Shipton; Silver Y;
Crimson-and-gold; Old Lady; Angle Shades.

II

And this is how darkness works: an alchemy
of chalk and silver, all our memories
of other gardens, distance, moonlit streams,
transformed to something punctual and slight,
flickering in the trap and only

guessed-at from the forms we sometimes glimpse
across a border, shapes we fail to name,
though they are bright and present, like a song,
their faces veined and hairstreaked in the gleam
that comes to meet us, when we turn for home.

III

Now I have been an amateur of light
for years, a surreptitious
builder in the dark of quiet snares,
to draw in from the air what it conceals,
nothing defined, but distance visible
as dancing flakes of life dusted with warmth
and pattern: echoes, sounding in my hands
or flaring at the windscreen on my journey
home each night, on deep lanes fledged with dusk,
while you are still receding in another
darkness, through torn hedgerows and a maze
of orchards, as the new moths catch and spark
on nothingness, arriving from the dark
at shapes and names, through light's pure dazzlement.

HEAT WAVE

After it rained, the back roads gusted with steam,
and the gardens along our street filled with the scent
of stocks and nicotiana,
but it didn't get properly hot till the night drew in,
humid and heavy as glass
on our well-kept lawn.
It was high in the summer. With everyone else
in town for the Lammas fair
I took the meadow-path to where the river
stalled on a sudden blackness: alders
shrouded in night and warmth, and the first slow owl
charting the further bank.

There was always movement there
beneath the slick of moonlight on the turning
water, like a life beneath the life
I understood as cattle tracks and birds:
a darker presence, rising from the stream,
to match my every move, my every breath.
Eel-black and cold, it melded in my flesh
with all the nooks and crannies of the world
where spawn appears, or changelings slip their skins
to ripen at the damp edge of the day,
still blurred with mud
and unrecovered song.

But that night, as the sky above me turned,
I found a different swimmer in the steady
shimmer of the tide,
a living creature, come from the other side
to slip into the cool
black water. I remember how she looked,
beneath the moon, so motiveless and white,

her body like a pod that had been shelled
and emptied: Mrs Pearce, my younger sister's
science teacher, turning in the lit
amazement of a joy that I could almost
smell, across the haze of drifting heat.

I was crouched beneath a stand
of willows and I guess she didn't see
the boy who watched her swim for half an hour
then turn for home beneath the August moon,
a half-smile on her face, her auburn hair
straggling and damp;
yet later, as I walked the usual streets,
I thought that she would stop and recognise
a fellow soul, with river in his eyes,
slipping home under a wave of light and noise,
and finding the key to her nights
in his soft, webbed fingers.

ANOTHER POEM ABOUT FISH

for Thomas Lynch

High tide;
        a seal in the harbour;
the water beyond the walls
                cursive and dark.

People come down to the rails
to watch and listen

drawn by a current
that runs to the edge of the world;

the fairy lights and rockabilly
fading at their backs
              the smell

of cigarettes and toffee
              and the shorefront's
blur of perpetual motion

paling against the fray
of a troubled sea.

And because he has heard the word
                      my son
repeats it when I raise him up and say

– pointing across the water –
                'Look:
a seal'

'A seal' he says;
                though not quite matching it
with what he knows from pictures
                                not quite

making it out
– the dog smile bobbing away
                                the air

a lattice of waves and movement
                                voices
blurring in the wind
                the fairground music

gusting across the water:
                        sweetness
and light

and never beneath it all
                        so much
as pulsing at its heart
                the shoals of fish

we know are out there
                strung across the firth
mile-deep and still
                or turning all at once

beyond what we know
as language
        and pledged to a moon

they alter
        with each sidestep
of the tide.

THE GRAVITY CHAIR

for Sarah

I used to think old age would be like this:
the afternoons more sudden than they are
in childhood, and the snow against the glass

more final, like the sports-announcer's voice
reading the football results while our neighbours' lights
quickened against the blackness out of doors.

I was seven, or seventeen, and I didn't know
how ageing works, like Zeno's paradox,
adjusting all the time, to right itself;

yet sometimes, on a winter's afternoon,
I thought of someone skilled – a juggler, say –
adapting to the pull of gravity

by shifts and starts, till something in the flesh
– a weightedness, a plumb-line to the earth –
revealed itself, consenting to be still.

DÜRER'S 'RHINOCERON'

This is the beast he imagines: sad
and dangerous, and so unlike itself
he gives it armour and an extra horn
to make it real.
                A hearsay animal,
it wavers at the edge of geometry
or recollects his own *Death and the Knight*;

and accurate is less than what he meant
by taking pen and ink, naming the parts,
and hatching deliberate shadows on the skull
and belly, like the darkness in the gaps
between the feathers of an angel's wing.

He never saw the creature for himself
but drew it from a sketch, or someone's
hazy recollection of the thing;
and though he must have heard the ship capsized
bringing it home, he never thought to draw
the slow fall through the water as it drowned,
craning its head to glimpse the savage light
of God's creation, locked in salt and sky.

THE EMPORIUM OF LIGHT

That story of Henry Miller's:
of how, when his wife cleared out

and left him with nothing,
not even a bed or a chair,

he bought himself
a pair of roller skates

and coasted from room to room
on the hardwood floor

for days, he said: bright
days of singleness.

Or something
even less

dramatic, taking
one thing at a time:

a life of chopping wood
and fetching water,

and nights in the roof of the house
when the town falls still;

the desk lamp burning,
gold against the glass,

but no reflection
– neither face, nor hands,

nor turning pages –
printed on the dark.

MILGRAM'S 'SHOCK GENERATOR'

It takes some time for everything to change
– the shadows on the ceiling look the same,
the smell of polish, windows blurred with rain –
but waking later, in another skin,
the man who understands, for the first time,
that he is lost, and everything is strange,

feels lucky. In the past he wanted more,
a half-shaped creature, waiting at a door
he should have opened; that he didn't dare
had more to do with memory than fear.
Now everything is as it was before,
but different – these instruments, this chair –
and someone talking in another room,
someone he loves, though nobody is there.

OF GRAVITY AND LIGHT

(lighthouse)

When mist forms over the firth
it slows the gulls that drift around the quay
to something like a standstill
                – only the barest
wingbeat troubles the air, the pearl and grey
of light becoming flesh, then vanishing.

You've reached the age for games that mimic flight:
lofted above my head, you are a stream
of giggles, though you know this joy depends
on something other than the trick it seems:
like everything that stalls, or gives us pause,
what we most love reveals itself as danger.

So let the mist come down, let there be haar,
long afternoons of drizzle, months of fog,
that we might know ourselves
                – such as we are –
a father and his child, out on the pier,
this weekday morning, guided by a star.

(Icarus)

The things that fall
are what we treasure most:

attendants
in the house of gravity

we sense the imminent
in every book

left open on a table
or a chair;

in every sugar bowl
or deck of cards

we understand
another life resides,

older than time
and dizzy with momentum;

yet, since the soul
is weightless, being neither

flesh and bone, nor shadow,
nor that sound

of falling in the distance
we mistake

for death,
or flight,

nothing is ever solid
in itself,

and substance
is another form of sleep

as feathers are,
no matter that the light

is still around a body
while it falls,

keeping it true, unhindered,
counterpoised,

something immense
to set against the pulse.

(blackbird)

It's not the space
between the cherry trees,

the angle of our smoke-house
or the sense

of something to be filled
above the lawn;

it's not the gaps
in matter, or the fear

of losing ground
that prompts him into song;

but, risen from the pull
of gravity,

the blackbird makes
a territory of light

and fills it with a sound
that feels, to us,

more fruit than stone, more
yolk than lacquered shell,

as if he knew
that nothing could endure

and relishes the fact,
calling the hen

to enter,
through the shadow he perfects

along the garden wall,
beneath the hedge,

in drainage pipes
and dead leaves shot with spore,

a kingdom for the earthbound
while we wait

for some new gaze
to reinvent the sky.

(enlightenment)

What we need most, we learn from the menial tasks:
the novice raking sand in Buddhist texts,
or sweeping leaves, his hands chilled to the bone,
while understanding hovers out of reach;
the changeling in a folk tale, chopping logs,
poised at the dizzy edge of transformation;

and everything they do is gravity:
swaying above the darkness of the well
to haul the bucket in; guiding the broom;
finding the body's kinship with the earth
beneath their feet, the lattice of a world
where nothing turns or stands outside the whole;

and when the insight comes, they carry on
with what's at hand: the gravel path; the fire;
knowing the soul is no more difficult
than water, or the fig tree by the well
that stood for decades, barren and inert,
till every branch was answered in the stars.

HISTORY

St Andrews: West Sands; September 2001

Today
     as we flew the kites
– the sand spinning off in ribbons along the beach
and that gasoline smell from Leuchars gusting across
the golf links;
              the tide far out
and quail-grey in the distance;
                            people
jogging, or stopping to watch
as the war planes cambered and turned
in the morning light –

today
     – with the news in my mind, and the muffled dread
of what may come –

                I knelt down in the sand
with Lucas
     gathering shells
and pebbles
     finding evidence of life in all this
driftwork:
     snail shells; shreds of razorfish;
smudges of weed and flesh on tideworn stone.

At times I think what makes us who we are
is neither kinship nor our given states
but something lost between the world we own
and what we dream about behind the names

on days like this
>   our lines raised in the wind
our bodies fixed and anchored to the shore

and though we are confined by property
what tethers us to gravity and light
has most to do with distance and the shapes
we find in water
>   reading from the book
of silt and tides
>   the rose or petrol blue
of jellyfish and sea anemone
combining with a child's
first nakedness.

Sometimes I am dizzy with the fear
of losing everything – the sea, the sky,
all living creatures, forests, estuaries:
we trade so much to know the virtual
we scarcely register the drift and tug
of other bodies
>   scarcely apprehend
the moment as it happens: shifts of light
and weather
>   and the quiet, local forms
of history: the fish lodged in the tide
beyond the sands;
>   the long insomnia
of ornamental carp in public parks
captive and bright
>   and hung in their own
slow-burning
>   transitive gold;
>   jamjars of spawn
and sticklebacks

                or goldfish carried home
from fairgrounds
            to the hum of radio

but this is the problem: how to be alive
in all this gazed-upon and cherished world
and do no harm

                a toddler on a beach
sifting wood and dried weed from the sand
and puzzled by the pattern on a shell

his parents on the dune slacks with a kite
plugged into the sky
                all nerve and line

patient; afraid; but still, through everything
attentive to the irredeemable.

III

WORLD

No: The world must be peopled.
　　William Shakespeare

BIRTH SONGS

Mutat enim mundi naturam totius aetas
Ex alioque alius status excipere omnia debet,
Nec manet ulla sui similis res. Omnia migrant.
                                                            Lucretius

I LULLABY

These are the days
of junk food at 4 a.m.

and night drives over the hill roads,
with your breathing

balanced between my fingers,
in the steering's

cartilage.
            I wonder what you dream

and whether dreams
are possible: what clouds of glory fade

to sunlight, daybreak,
hints of gorse and tar.

And nothing is more mysterious
than here:

this morning,
when we venture from the road

into a realm of shades
and fairy rings,

to claim this negative
of grass and night,

where rabbits scatter
from our turning light,

and, somewhere in the grass,
an insect sings.

II MULTIPLE BIRTH

He came alone. No shadow in the scan
of someone else; no soft, insistent gleam
between the vertebrae, or at the rim
of light and sound. A single, human form:
our only son; our firstborn; no one's twin;
sole epicentre of the local storm
that glimmered into substance in your womb.
And yet, this morning, when you went to town,
we sat together in the downstairs room,
certain, but not convinced we were alone;
nothing was wrong, and when I picked him up
the house was still; the windows full of sky.
Cradled against my chest, he fell asleep,
but, somewhere in the roof, I heard him cry.

III PROMENADE

In your third month, the last of the summer
is cut grass, and mist in the wynds,
and that half-life of fishbone and hair
by the harbour wall;

and on our daily walks between
the seafront and the slow fade of the park,
I scout the narrow roads and chandlers' yards
for coils of light and pools of gravity,

faint patterns that remind me of a world
I learned by shifts and starts over the months
we thought of you as waterborne: a boat
suspended in the starlight of the womb.

I'm saying this to someone years away,
a man I've never met, and cannot know,
another mind, an awkward, vivid self,
with memories of other days than this,

but somewhere in it all, there has to be –
amidst the smudged allure of parents' things
and waking early in a stranger's house
to lie alone, while darkness turns to light –

there has to be a morning much like this:
a broken hull the colour of old rye;
abandoned boats; wet rope; a pagan wind
etching the harbour wall with salt and sky.

IV GYMNASIUM 1522

Because what I choose to believe
is that something will show —
a glimmer between the lines of transmigration;
rain in the hallway; a child's face turned to the sky
and filling with light;
that perfect scent of glycerine and ink
breeding between my fingers like a sign —

three hours from home, in Moscow, when the driver
loses his way in the sidestreets and stops
to ask for directions,
the half-road blurring with leaves and running out
between each crossroads and the next in pools of rain
that have thickened and stalled for days
through the summer's waning —

three hours from home, while you wake in the early dark,
a woman is pointing the way down a muddy lane
and the car hurries on to where a suburban school
sits nestled amongst the trees, the house I expected
diminishing into concrete and clouded glass,
and the patches of mud and gravel in the driveway
sweetened with fallen apples, sycamore, the last

cornflower blue of a daybreak I half-imagine
as something from a folk-tale or a song
that women sing to children, when the night
takes shape and lingers, blue-black and incomplete,
between a clouded doorway and the blur
of laundry and painted eggs and the smell of ash
where kinship begins and ends, though we call it time.

V QUICKSAND

When the penny dropped from my hand
and settled, the blackened face
of Georgivs Rex dissolving in the sand,

I saw how lovingly the earth resumes
possession, like a blizzard in reverse,
retaining every blemish, every scratch

and fingerprint, a history of touch
and currency, laid down
and buried with that last faint bloom of warmth

unwittingly surrendered to a depth
I thought about for days, through paper rounds
and chemistry exams, as it became

the echo of my ordinary self
sounded-out and guessed-at in a chill
descent that would continue while I walked

from home to school, from school to morning mass:
another presence, folding through the long
slow water, like a descant, or a pulse.

VI CATALOGUE

Because we need a history of lilac,
of all the late spring mornings when the house
is open to the air, the floors and sills
dusted with light and pollen

                      and because
no cherry trees are pictured in those maps
we learned to draw in school, blocking the land
with pencil-marks, or crayon, or the red
of conquest;

              for the children we have never quite
abandoned, and because you are our child,
we sit up late, till midnight, choosing shrubs
to grow between the smokehouse and the wall

– spiraea, mallow, buckthorn, guelder rose –
near-native plants, that anyone might trust
to bloom, in time, like bodies, or the shapes
an apple makes, before it falls to earth.

KITH

for Gemma

The way it tastes of the past
when the house is empty;

or how we think ourselves alone,
remembering the beauty in a look
we cannot place;

the feel of our own
slow warmth, on an afternoon

when the hum of traffic stops and the blackbird
recovers the map it had made
of the hedges and trees;

the sense of time not passing, as we pass
through time and space

is something like the light that stands between
a man and a woman,
a woman a man and a child.

Though what we know is mostly the agreed
and measured, what we are is something else

and never comes
without some inattention:
light on a kitchen wall, light on a face,

a truth that resides
in the details: the ebb and flow

of seasons
and the world we paraphrase
as crease and furrow; grass-blade; robin's nest;

the *terra incognita* of the whole.

ON KVALOYA

Die Sprache der Natur ist einer geheimen Losung zu vergleichen,
die jeder Posten dem nächsten in seiner eigenen Sprache weitergibt,
der Inhalt der Losung aber ist die Sprache des Postens selbst.
Walter Benjamin

I LEARNING TO TALK

This is our game for now, rehearsing words
to make the world seem permanent, and ours;
before it disappears, I will have named
all we can see, from here to the snow on Kvannfjellet,
the yarrow in the grass, a passing swan,
eider and black-backed gull at the rim of the sound.

I gloss uncertainties – this lime-green weed
that fetches up a yard above the tide;
those seabirds in the channel, too far out
to call for sure; these unspecific moths;
a chequered wagtail, similar enough,
though different, to those we know at home.

It never ends; there's always something else:
a single blackbird quietly arrives
from nowhere, at the far edge of the lawn
and everything we know is strange again,
the daylight turned to gloaming on the fields,
your face a maze of sleep and inattention.

Coming indoors, the house is still as glass;
a half-read book lies open on the table.
Later, you'll sleep and dream of something else,
a seamless order, dark with flight and tides,
a silence to replace my questing voice,

but I'll go out at midnight in a haze
of moths and pollen, on the Hella road,
finding and naming, one thing at a time:
fieldfare, redshank, cranesbill, alchemilla.

II METAMORPHOSIS

If, when the story ends, we are transformed
to something else: new memories and tastes
arriving from the dark and suddenly
familiar, like the strangers in a dream,

new eyes to see the world, another light
unfolding in another type of brain,
a foreign tongue for mimicry or song,
frogskin or petals, swansdown or living fur,

if we return to what we cannot lose
as anything at all, let us be moths
and wander in the certainties of grass
and buttercups, unsure of what we are,
but ready, for as long as time allows,
to fill the meadows with a new becoming.

III TERN

Four days of wind;
a black cloud
over Malangen.

The eider
squabble and drowse
in the fleeting rain.

I've heard it said:
we are
what we imagine;

but just now,
turning for home,
I caught the storm

shaping a bird
from the swerve
of the not-yet-seen.

IV JAIN

I was walking back over the meadows,
the light off Malangen silver, all of a sudden,
and cold, like the light off a mirror
or polished stone.

The terns were feeding out along the shore,
hovering over the sound like holograms,
and something was moving away
in the windless grass,

an animal perhaps,
some frightened thing
I sensed, but couldn't see,
a yard away.

I stopped dead: in a clump of buttercups
a creature stirred; then far out in the grass
another wave, until I realised
that everything was moving, one long tide

of animals
in flight from where I stood,
and for that moment, I was powerless,
afraid to move, inept, insensible.

Of course, I imagined it all,
as we only imagine
ghosts, or a stranger's hand
at the base of the spine,

but for a minute
I was not alone,

the meadow bright
and motionless again,

the slow fall in my bones
correcting now,
less balanced, than attuned,
to gravity.

A DUCK ISLAND FLORA

for Michael Longley

On the road to the Brensholmen ferry:
snow gentians, mineral blue
and perfect, like a child's idea of north;

but here is all marshland
and water between the fields
where they still cut and rake the hay
with tools that are heirlooms.

Two types of bog-cotton grow:
torvull and *duskull*;
and lady's mantle: *Alchemilla mollis*;
marikåpe.

On the high road, over the pass,
there are purple orchids;
but close to town
a common beauty thrives:

cornflowers; bluebells; dogwood; purple vetch;
kornblomst; blåklokke; skrubbaer; fuglevikke.

BLEIK

What there is to see
is mostly sky:
small rain and that blanched light off the sand
that gives the town its name, the word in Norwegian,
bleik, meaning 'ghostly' or 'pale'
and not what we thought.
The tourist guides speak mostly of the climate,
glacial moraine and the green ridge circling the town
no more than a backdrop
for windstorms and midnight sun.
It's mostly seascapes or the northern lights
in the handful of postcards they sell in the only store
where locals gather for coffee, the old men
rehearsing the parallel lines of a conversation
that might have run for years, while the friendly assistant
rings up our order and shows, with a shake of the head,
that she understands nothing is here
but daylight and sky.

Yet everything is here
that we could need:
a main street with a sports club and a church;
a cottage roofed with turf, its garden
narrow and trim, with lilac and meconopsis.
Children play tag beside the old-fashioned
diesel pump that someone has painted
buttercup yellow, although it is no longer used
and hasn't worked for years.
Out on the beach you can find an assortment of weeds,
cold-water corals, sandflies, splinters of bone,
feathers and charcoal, fragments of *kråkebolle*.
The houses are sky white, or ochre,
navy, or powder blue with rust-brown lintels,

and two streets up from the shore, on Laksebakkveien,
someone has filled a window with coloured lights.

On a good day
the water is turquoise.
Waves of shore birds flow along the headland,
avoiding the one stray cat in a labyrinth
of dune grass and those pale, mouse-scented plants
the people here call 'dog cakes'.
The gulls and crows that wander on the beach
look playful, or bright, and gather in congregation,
as if there is something they know about the world
that we have not quite grasped.
On a good day, the light is resumed;
a low wind sings in the power lines edging the road
to the Aurora Borealis
Research Base;
but this is the season where one thing blends with another,
clouds on the skerries, or figments of summer light
in the quickening clouds.
A boy stands on his own beside the fish house.
We know he's a local, just from the set of his eyes.
He might have been here for decades, watching the tide,
no more or less responsive than the gulls
to what the wind blows in, or strips away.
A woman in a blue and yellow skirt
carries her shopping home and sets it down
by the gate to the turf-covered house, while she finds her key
and lets herself in.

Later, when we pass this way again,
she will come to the door, and the stairs will be lit behind her,
warm with that glow we learn from picture books
in childhood, learn
from radio and first love and defeat,

as migrant birds will learn an estuary,
not to recall, but to know, when it comes again,
as somewhere to feed, or shelter, or avoid,
just as we know this moment, if not by name,
then by some trace of atmosphere or warmth:
a glimpse of something, not quite what we thought,
but just enough, that we can think of home
in this, the most provisional of worlds.

BLACKBIRD

(dream catcher)

It's not the bird itself,
but what it does

— the vanishing —
is what we come to learn;

though nothing in the day
feels different:

the usual morning
      street trees   lighted yards
the noise of traffic   out beyond the point

and hanging in the grey
above our bed
a knot of wire and feathers
        scarlet twine
and crazing

    — they said we were born with souls
    and I thought of something paper-white
    and empty, like the sweet communion host
    that melted on my tongue, and left no trace —

and still, when the blackbird returns,
we step outside and leave the door ajar
the colour and perfume of lilies blurring the walls
the shadow that stands in the hallway

    — a song, a guide —

sweeter by far than anything we know.

(in a green light)

That history we never learned in school,
where living things are born into their names
as easily as morning fills a room,

and sleep is deeper than the sleep we share
with trees and insects, deeper than the wind
that gusts along the coast road after rain.

And when we speak of once upon a time,
I always think a sound is all we have
to go on, like that echo in the well

behind the church: a secret memory
unfolding in our hearts, while we pursue
this other life, this common frequency.

We know the scent of lilac and the chill
of falling water; clouds above the town
and cradles stopped with salt, or herringbone.

We know a world
– and still we live untouched,
hiding our love in the dark, with rags and shells,

or thinking of the games we played
as children, in the green of afternoon,
tossing a ball back and forth, on an open field,

the air turning soft and cool above the park
the darkness seeping in
through autumn trees;

how, all the time, we wanted to go on,
in tune with every move, alert and spare,
watching the ball as it travelled from hand to hand,

our bodies skilled and warming to a loss
as total and incomplete
as a blackbird's singing.

(metempsychosis)

Who would be born again in the plated flesh
of the armadillo?
              An old conquistador
gone native, and snuffling for gold
through scrubland, or broken stones?

Who would return in a body of fish-scale or fur?
The carp in its sleeve of mud, or a wintered bear
immersed in the varieties of sleep,
a dream of frost, a snowfall's blurred caesura?

And who would ask for anything but this:
a quiet in the middle of the day,
the bird table scattered with peanuts and scraps of rind,
the hedge trees white with snow beyond the fence?

All afternoon, the blackbird comes and goes,
returning the shade that glimmers in the blood
to a silence between the trees
and the winter sky,

and shall I follow, taking up the life
that waits to happen: creature memories
and blood-heat; colours; stitchwork in the bones;
the singsong heart that beats amongst the leaves?

Or shall I say, before it slips my mind,
and though I understood, when love began,
that love is always threaded with forgetting
– always the light from the pier in a childhood dream

or those rooms where we lived for a summer
before moving on,
the half-finished jar of honey, the spice-rack and echoes
sealed in an empty kitchen against the snow –

before the bird returns, shall I refuse
all comfort from the notion of rebirth,
unless the voice you carry to the dark
resumes where it left off, and I can listen.

(entremonde)

In all those childhood tales of transformation —
of huntsmen turned to ice, or pools of blood,

or dreaming girls, awakened with a kiss,
becoming trees, or gone into the shapes

of seals;
       in all those stories we would tell
around a fire, or gathered in the dark,

isn't the best the one where the children find
a borderline between their mother's world

and somewhere else?
— a hidden cave, perhaps,

or some enchanted house beside the sea
where spirits walk, in clouds of song and light,

and blue is something tangible, like snow?
We've been there once or twice, I think, by now,

moving from room to room, or walking out
together, in a dawn sky packed with stars,

and even if we never turn again
to where the blackbird waits, amongst the leaves,

we know the lines to cross, the hidden tracks
that sing beneath the holly brakes and springs;

and even if we stay within these bounds
for years, between the dance hall and the kirk,

or sit indoors, while snow falls on the woods
a mile away, we know that someone else

will pick the story up, where we left off,
and go on speaking, softly, to the air.

AFTER LUCRETIUS

Nam quodcumque suis mutatum finibus exit,
Continuo hoc mors est illius quod fuit ante.
                                    Lucretius

I

It happens from time to time,
on days like this

– in winter, when the air is cold
and still,

the boats at the harbour
perched on their wooden stocks,

the gaps between the houses
filled with light –

it happens that I think of all
the vanishings I learned about in childhood:

that ship they found at sea,
unanchored, blind,

the table set for lunch, the galley
filling with steam;

the blank of the lamp-room
at Flannan, where they found

no sign of the men
who were waiting to be relieved;

the boy from a northern village, going out
at daybreak, to get kindling for a fire,

a line of footprints
stopping in the woods

and gradually erased
by morning snow.

When they speak about angels in books,
I think what they mean is this sudden

arrival at somewhere else
through a rift in the fabric,

this glimpse of the absence that forms
between two lives

– and it comes as no surprise, on days like this,
alone in the house, or walking on the shore

at evening, that I'll stop dead and recall
the disappearances my childhood self

never quite engineered,
or how it is a legend in these parts

that one bright afternoon,
in wintertime,

something will come from nowhere
and touch a man

for no good reason; ice-cold on his skin
or sharp as a needle,

it finds him and moves away
and leaves no mark.

It's not what he expected, neither death
nor absolution, but a slow and painless

fall between the collarbone and wrist
that lasts for days,

and when he disappears,
amidst the thaw,

there is nothing to show he is missing,
not even

II

    an absence.

Though each thing dies
into its own becoming,
the shed skin falling away,
still beautiful:

an empty form,
but governed by the moon,
like bone,
or thaw;

and if we are the fleshed
and perishable shadows of a soul
that shifts and slides
beneath this everyday

appearance, we are bound
by greenness and decay to see ourselves
each in the other, staying
and turning aside,

as lovers do, unable to resist
this ebb and flow:
new animals, with nothing in their minds
but light and air,

the creatures
of a sudden mystery,
who hurry on
towards the difficult;

III

though never the plural:
                              high barns filled with straw
and the flicker of errant birds
amongst the rafters,

a quiet fish-house, open to the sun,
where the packers sit turned from their work
to smoke or talk,

a litter of gut and ice
on the wet stone floor
catching the light,

or any schoolyard where the children wheel
and turn from their games
as if catching a sound in the distance

and waiting to hear it swell, to make it out:
a noise like water, say,
or gathered birds

far in the almost-heard, in the almost known,
is where it happens, singular and large
and unremarkable, like ice, or fire.

IV

Thirteen months of driving back and forth
across the sound:

the old reds and gunpowder blues
of tethered boats

or long-legged waders
stepping away through the mist

remembered as something
platonic.
         What we know

is never quite the sum
of what we find,

moving towards a light
we only half

imagine: salt-dreams
printed in the flesh,

the echo of other bodies we have borne
through blizzards, silence, unrequited loves

and always that foreign self, who never leaves
the middle-ground

yet never fully
hoves into view:

a blur at the edge of the print,
that might be human:

a single
time-lapsed suggestion

of movement, that could just as easily
be something else:

a litter of rags, perhaps,
or a tended fire,

and just as we see the differing
versions of grey in the offing

as woodsmoke, or the unexpected gap
where nothing happening becomes

the drama, so we find
no space for Icarus to fall

and vanish
at the blue edge of the world,

only the usual story of some
local, who went out one afternoon

and strayed home decades later, much the same
as when he left: a story with a point

you couldn't miss,
or so it would appear,

living amongst your kind
in towns like this,

where truth is always local, like the thought
that comes to mind, as winter closes in,

a thought you guard against for years
until you guess

that nothing matters less
than being seen.

VIRIDITAS

for Andy Brown and Amy Shelton

I

*Et illa apparuerunt omnia
in viriditate plena*

It's the green you can still make out
       in antique
photographs: those unexpected depths
in black and white.

Though it's best
       when you don't understand
the word in itself,
catching the hint of leaf
in a map or a place-name.

Think of the bloom on a plum
       or how a stem
of dogwood or upland cherry will have stood
for months in its sheath of ice
       before the sun.

Think of these living ossuaries of oak
       and shadow
or those headstones locked in moss,
the old names lodged in green, forever
       unrepeatable.

It's buried in the flesh
with avocet and lizard and the last

    glimmer of rock-salt
        ravelled in the spine,

but never think it;
    let it go unnamed:
a ghost of xylem, flexed against the blood,
or some damp windfall
        bletting in the bone.

II

Et protegis viridi rore

Call it decay, but the first
glimmer of autumn is sweetness:

that glycerine trail
on the path to the arboretum,

the crushed-plum and rainwater scent
in the outer fence.

And all we know of windfalls
is the key

to whiteness:
a decipherment of snow

as sanctuary, new
sugars in the blood

that cannot be erased
by sleet or frost

or wholly interrupted
by a thaw.

III

*O tener flos campi,
et o dulcis viriditas pomi,
et o sarcina sine medulla*

Late in the year
we remember to watch for snow

as if coming to something new
like a birth, or silence.

It's not what we expect
to be redeemed

so easily by what we most neglect;
but somewhere in the gap between

the last faint gust of birchseed and the point
where rain is blue again

something like guesswork
happens amongst the leaves

that rot in drifts against
the outhouse wall,

to quicken in our bonfires:
single

threads of sycamore
and blackened rain

becoming mildew, slut's hair,
random birds.

IV

De te nubes fluunt,
ether volat,
lapides humorem habent,
aque rivulos educent,
et terra viriditatem sudat

We might return one day
from black and white:

snow on our boots, and an old song
clear in our minds,

the smell of distance clinging to our hands
like wintersweet.

We always wondered
how the self persists

through sleep and memory
and blinding fear,

how all those shapes
that flicker in the dark

leave us uninterrupted, like the green
of holly leaves, or ivy, or the medieval

stillness of a hedgerow, in the haze
of middle-ground

where those we might have been
go on forever, lost in wonderment.

A THEORY OF EVERYTHING

Until it deals with gravity and light
and how they loose and bind
all the ten thousand things

I'll settle for that reach of sunlit track
that led out to the sea

at Mirtiotissa:

the sound of water rushing through the pines
towards us   and a scent

unfolding from the earth, to draw us in

– a history of light
and gravity   – no more –

for this is how the world
occurs: not piecemeal
                        but entire
and instantaneous

the way we happen:

woman   blackbird   man